NORWEGIAN FJORDS CRUISE

TRAVEL GUIDE 2024-2025

An Essential Companion To Sailing Through Majestic Landscapes, Hidden Gems, and Timeless Nordic Traditions

Cedric J. Stone

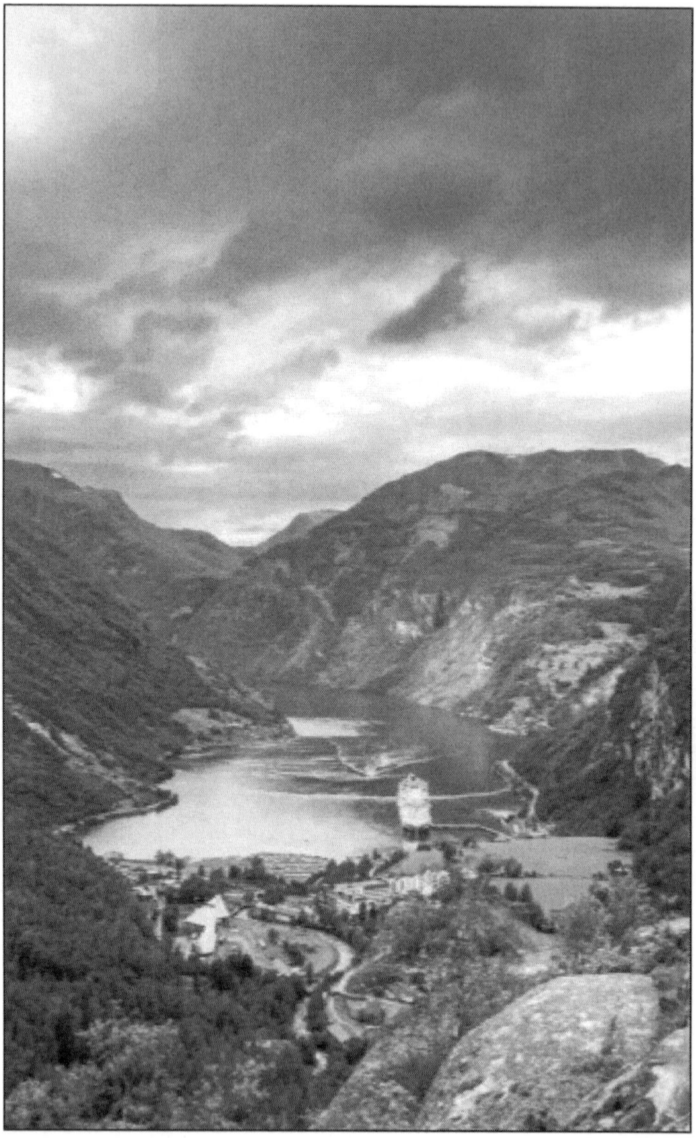

COPYRIGHT

All rights reserved. No part of this publication may be reproduced, distributed, or transmitted in any form or by any means, including photocopying, recording, or other electronic or mechanical methods, without the prior written permission of the publisher, except in the case of brief quotations embodied in critical reviews and certain other non-commercial uses permitted by copyright law.

Copyright © 2024 by Cedric J. Stone

TABLE OF CONTENTS

Gratitude 6

INTRODUCTION 11

    Welcome To The Norwegian Fjords 11

    Why Cruise Through the Norwegian Fjords in 2024-2025 13

    How to Use This Guide 15

    Quick Facts About The Norwegian Fjords 17

CHAPTER ONE 21

    Planning Your Cruise 21

    Selecting the Right Cruise Line and Ship 22

    Booking and Travel Arrangements 24

    What to Pack: Essentials for your Cruise 25

    Embarkation: What to Expect 27

CHAPTER TWO 29

    Getting There and Around 29

    Reaching Norway 30

    Getting To The Cruise Departure Port 32

    Navigating The Fjords 34

    Tips For Navigating The Fjords 37

CHAPTER THREE 39

    Accommodation On Board 39

Cabin Types and Categories..40

Considerations For Choosing A Cabin.......................................44

Onboard Activities and Entertainment................................. 46

CHAPTER FOUR..**49**

Ports of Call and Excursions...49

Bergen: Gateway to the Fjords... 50

Geirangerfjord, Nature's Masterpiece..52

Flåm: A Village of Natural Wonders..54

Stavanger: A Combination of Old and New........................... 56

Ålesund: An Art Nouveau Gem... 58

CHAPTER FIVE.. **61**

Dining and Cuisine... 61

The Foundation of Norwegian Cuisine...................................62

Traditional Norwegian Dishes..63

Five Budget-Friendly Restaurants in the Norwegian Fjords.......68

CHAPTER SIX..**79**

Events and Festivals...79

National Celebrations.. 80

Music and Art Festivals.. 82

Historical and Cultural Festivals.. 85

Food and Beverage Festivals.. 87

Seasonal and Outdoor Events...88

CHAPTER SEVEN... **91**

Practical Information.. 91

Currency and Payment Methods... 92

Language and Communication..93

Health and Safety.. 95

Traveling With Children... 96

BONUS SECTION... **97**

Sample Itineraries..97

Seasonal Recommendations...105

Basic Norwegian Phrases... 113

Shopping and Souvenirs in The Norwegian Fjords................ 116

Gratitude

Dear Readers,

Thank you for choosing this book to guide you on your next adventure. Your interest and curiosity are greatly appreciated, and I am grateful for the chance to share the beauties of our world with you. Before you begin the adventures detailed within these pages, I'd like to express my heartfelt gratitude.

Your support means everything to me, and I am confident that this book will be a valuable companion on your journey. Whether you're planning your first vacation or returning to uncover new treasures, you'll find inspiration, practical insights, and a greater bond with the places you visit.

Enjoy every second of your journey, and may your memories be as breathtaking as the sights you will see.

Thank you for your participation in our adventure.

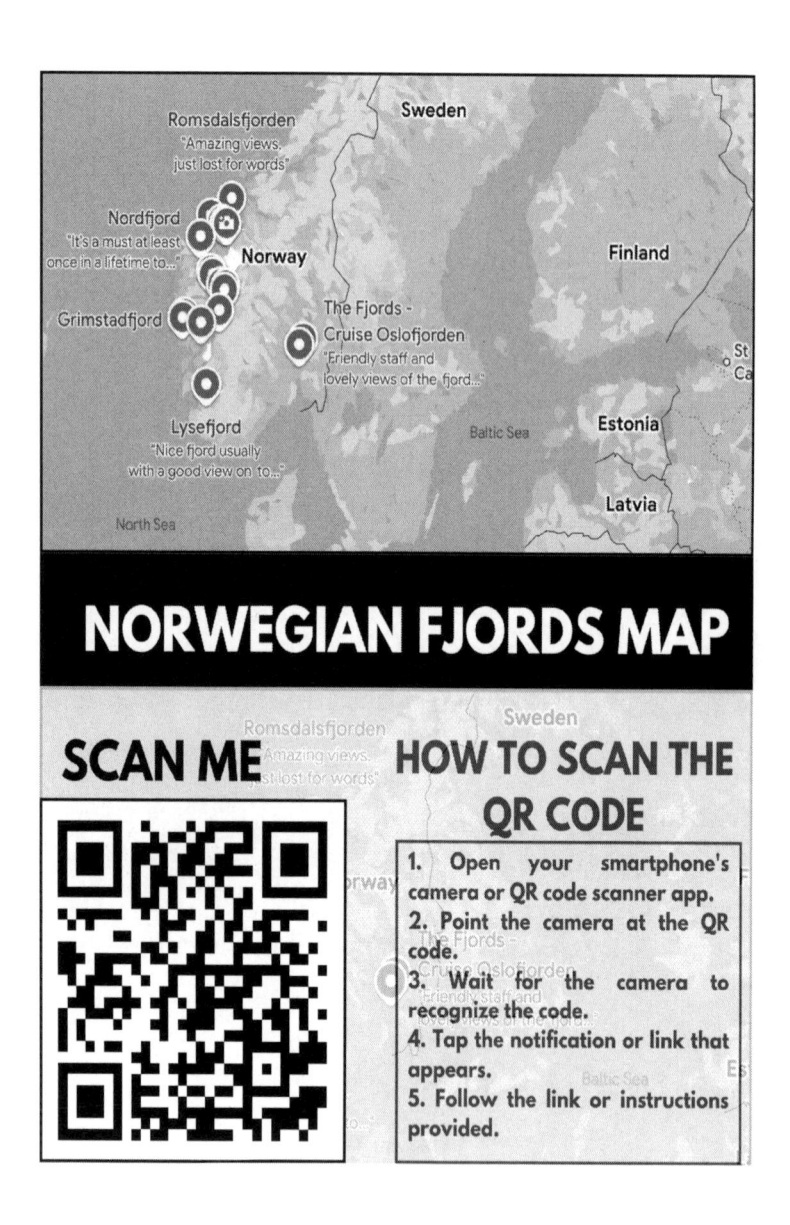

NORWEGIAN FJORDS MAP

Romsdalsfjorden — "Amazing views, just lost for words"

Nordfjord — "It's a must at least once in a lifetime to..."

Grimstadfjord — "Friendly staff and lovely views of the fjord..."

The Fjords - Cruise Oslofjorden — "Friendly staff and lovely views of the fjord..."

Lysefjord — "Nice fjord usually with a good view on to..."

SCAN ME

HOW TO SCAN THE QR CODE

1. Open your smartphone's camera or QR code scanner app.
2. Point the camera at the QR code.
3. Wait for the camera to recognize the code.
4. Tap the notification or link that appears.
5. Follow the link or instructions provided.

8 | NORWEGIAN FJORDS CRUISE TRAVEL GUIDE

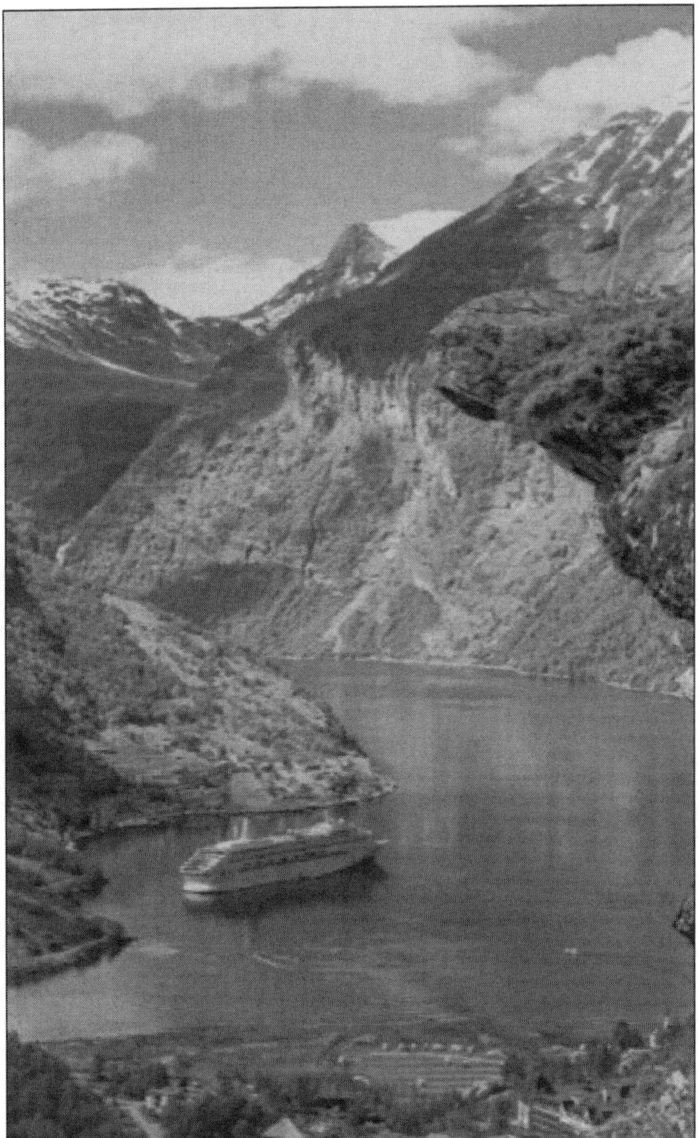

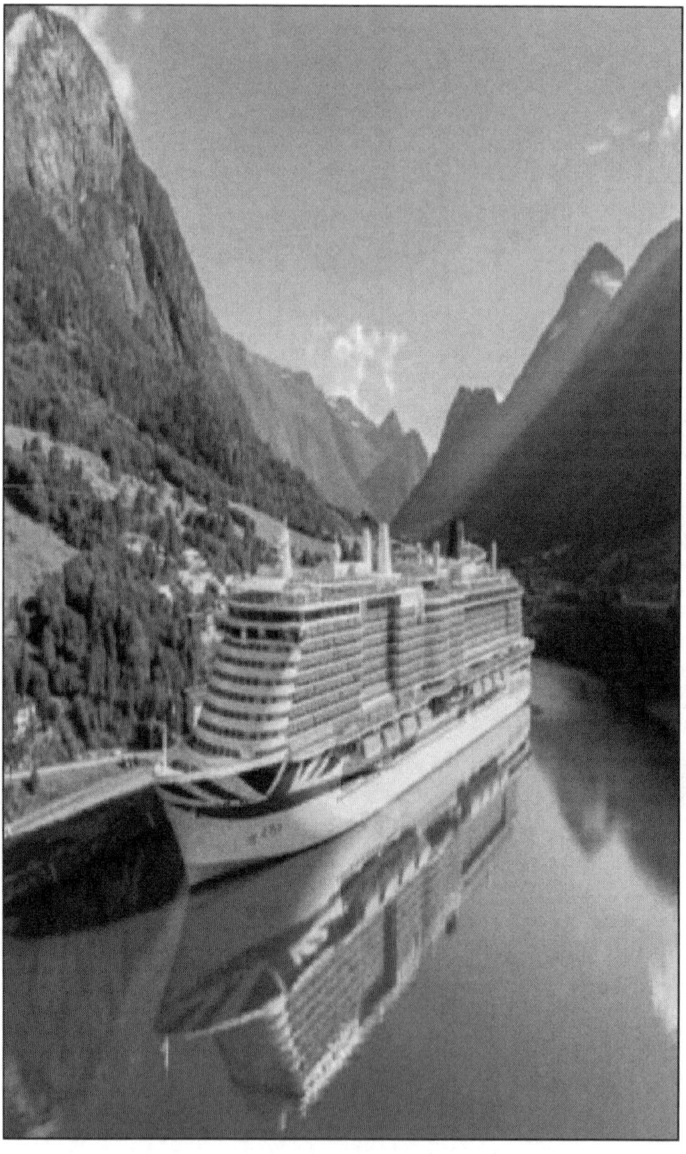

INTRODUCTION

Welcome To The Norwegian Fjords

The Norwegian fjords are awe-inspiring natural wonders, famed for their spectacular scenery, clear waterways, and rich cultural heritage. These fjords, located along Norway's western coast, have captivated visitors for ages with their breathtaking majesty and distinct charm. This introduction will take you on a tour through the appeal of the fjords, explaining why they are a must-see destination and how they form an ideal setting for an unforgettable cruise.

The Allure of The Fjords

The Norwegian fjords are more than just a spectacular physical feature; they demonstrate the strength and beauty of nature. These deep, narrow sea inlets were carved by glaciers during the last Ice Age and are surrounded by towering cliffs and beautiful surroundings. The fjords run from the North Sea to the Arctic Circle, providing a range of experiences from peaceful and relaxing to harsh and daring.

Scenic Beauty

The fjords provide some of the most breathtaking scenery in the world. Imagine drifting across tranquil waterways surrounded by steep, forested mountains and gushing waterfalls. Each fjord has its own distinct personality, from the serene serenity of the Geirangerfjord to the immense expanses of the Sognefjord, often known as the "King of the Fjords." This breathtaking environment offers endless options for photography and simply taking in the natural beauty.

Why Cruise Through the Norwegian Fjords in 2024-2025

Cruising through the Norwegian fjords in 2024-2025 offers a once-in-a-lifetime experience, blending breathtaking landscapes with rich cultural heritage. The fjords, carved by glaciers over thousands of years, are an awe-inspiring sight with towering cliffs, cascading waterfalls, and tranquil waters. A cruise allows you to immerse yourself in this natural beauty while visiting picturesque coastal towns like Bergen, Geiranger, and Flam, each steeped in history and charm.

One of the best reasons to cruise the fjords is the unique perspective it offers. You can glide through the serene waters, passing landscapes that are often inaccessible by road. The contrast of the deep blue fjords against lush green mountains, capped by snow in the cooler months, creates a mesmerizing backdrop for your journey.

2024-2025 is an ideal time to embark on this adventure. Norway's cruise industry has taken significant steps toward sustainability, using eco-friendly ships and reducing environmental impact. Additionally, you'll enjoy seasonal highlights like the Midnight Sun in summer, where daylight stretches for nearly 24 hours, or the magical Northern Lights during the fall and winter months.

From the incredible scenery to the chance to witness wildlife such as eagles, seals, and whales, a Norwegian fjords cruise in 2024-2025 promises an unforgettable experience. It's the perfect blend of nature, culture, and adventure, making it a top choice for travelers seeking something truly extraordinary.

How to Use This Guide

Welcome to an immersive Norwegian Fjords Cruise Travel Experience. Whether you're a first-time cruiser or a seasoned traveler, this guide is designed to help you make the most of your Norwegian fjords adventure. Here's how to navigate the sections and maximize your experience:

Getting Started: Begin by familiarizing yourself with the "Planning Your Cruise" section. Here, you'll find essential tips on choosing the right cruise line, itinerary, and cabin type to suit your preferences and budget. We've also included information on the best time to visit, what to pack, and how to prepare for your trip.

Exploring the Fjords: Each chapter is dedicated to a specific region or fjord, providing in-depth information on must-see destinations like Geirangerfjord, Bergen, and Flåm. You'll discover the best shore excursions, local attractions, and cultural highlights, along with insider tips to help you experience each destination like a local.

Dining and Cuisine: Norwegian cuisine is an essential part of your journey. Our "Dining and Cuisine" sections provide suggestions for traditional dishes to try, both on board and during shore excursions. We've also included dietary tips and restaurant recommendations to help you savor the local flavors.

Practical Information: In the "Practical Information" section, you'll find useful details on everything from currency exchange and tipping to language basics and Wi-Fi access onboard. These tips will ensure a smooth trip and help you navigate both the cruise and the local culture effortlessly.

Itineraries: Lastly, don't miss the "Itineraries" section, where we've outlined suggested trips based on different preferences and timeframes. Whether you have a weekend or a full week, this section provides a variety of options for all types of travelers.

Dive in and enjoy planning your unforgettable Norwegian fjords cruise!

Quick Facts About The Norwegian Fjords

The Norwegian fjords are among the world's most outstanding natural attractions, with beautiful scenery, distinct geological features, and a rich cultural heritage. These fjords, which are deep, glacially sculpted valleys filled with seawater, are a tribute to nature's enormous power and have enthralled visitors for ages. Here are a few basic facts about these wonderful natural wonders:

Climate and Weather

The Gulf Stream influences the climate in the Norwegian fjords, resulting in a relatively moderate environment when compared to other locations at similar latitudes. Summers are normally cool, with temperatures ranging from 10 to 20 degrees Celsius (50 to 68 degrees Fahrenheit), while winters are moderate and damp, with temperatures hanging around 0 degrees Celsius (32°F). This mild climate supports lush greenery and rich fauna along the fjords.

Rainfall is abundant, especially in the fall and winter, adding to the region's lush foliage and numerous waterfalls. The fjords are home to some of Europe's tallest waterfalls, notably the Seven Sisters and the Bridal Veil in Geirangerfjord, which flow impressively from the cliffs into the fjord waters.

Human History and Culture

Humans have lived in the fjord regions for thousands of years, drawn by the abundant natural resources and fertile soil. Archaeological evidence indicates that the first residents came around 6,000 years ago, creating villages focused on fishing, farming, and trading. The fjords were important trading routes for the Vikings, who used them to discover, trade, and conquer distant areas.

Today, the fjords are home to scenic villages and small towns where traditional Norwegian culture and customs are preserved. Agriculture, particularly fruit cultivation, is important to the local economy, with the Hardangerfjord region well-known for its apple and cherry orchard. Explore the picturesque hamlet of Flåm, Balestrand, and Olden, where wooden cottages with sod roofs and colorful gardens create idyllic settings.

Sustainability and Conservation
The Norwegian fjords are a UNESCO World Heritage Site, demonstrating its extraordinary natural beauty and cultural value. Efforts to protect natural environments are top priorities for both local communities and the government. Norway is committed to sustainable tourism methods, which maintain the natural environment while allowing visitors to enjoy the fjords responsibly.

Initiatives include limiting cruise ship traffic in specific locations, promoting eco-friendly accommodations, and encouraging the use of electric vehicles and public transportation to cut carbon emissions. Visitors are asked to follow the "Leave No Trace" principles, which reduce their environmental impact by respecting wildlife, properly disposing of rubbish, and staying on designated paths and trails.

CHAPTER ONE

Planning Your Cruise

Planning a cruise through the Norwegian fjords is a wonderful excursion in and of itself, with numerous options and considerations that can significantly enhance your experience. The planning step, which includes everything from choosing the proper cruise company to deciding when to go, sets the setting for an outstanding experience. Here is a comprehensive guide to navigating this vital step and ensuring that your fjord cruise is everything you hoped for.

Selecting the Right Cruise Line and Ship

The first step in organizing your Norwegian fjords trip is to choose the cruise line and ship that best suit your interests and expectations. Various cruise lines provide fjord itineraries, each with their own set of features and amenities.

Major Cruise Lines:

- **Hurtigruten:** Also known as the "Norwegian Coastal Express," Hurtigruten provides an authentic and immersive experience that highlights Norwegian culture and nature. Their ships are smaller, allowing them to travel to tight fjords and lesser-known ports.
- **Norwegian Cruise Line (NCL):** Provides larger ships with a variety of onboard amenities, including several dining options, entertainment, and family activities. NCL offers a more resort-like experience while highlighting the fjords' beauty.
- **Celebrity Cruises:** Celebrity Cruises is known for its opulent accommodations and exquisite meals, catering to travelers looking

for a more upmarket experience. They provide extensive itineraries centered on comfort and style.
- **Royal Caribbean:** It provides huge ships with novel amenities like rock climbing walls and ice skating rinks. They are great for travelers who want to combine fjord exploration with a variety of onboard entertainment options.

Factors to Consider:

- **Size of the Ship:** Consider the size of the ship, as smaller ships can cross narrower fjords and visit less accessible ports, providing a more intimate experience. Larger ships offer greater facilities, but their ability to enter certain fjords may be limited.
- **Onboard Amenities:** Consider what amenities are vital to you, such as restaurants, entertainment, spa services, and fitness centers.
- **Target Audience:** Some cruises are geared toward families, while others focus on luxury or adventure travel. Choose a line that matches your travel style.

- **Duration of Cruise:** Norwegian fjord cruises typically last from 5 to 14 days. Determine how much time you want to spend at sea and how many ports you'd like to visit.

Booking and Travel Arrangements

Once you've decided on your cruise line, ship, and travel dates, it's time to make your reservation and organize the logistics of your vacation.

Booking Tips:

- **Early Booking:** To get the best pricing and your desired stateroom type, book your trip as soon as possible, particularly for summer departures.
- **Discount and Promotions:** Keep a lookout for early bird bargains, group discounts, and promotional offers. Booking through a travel agent may provide access to exclusive deals.
- **Cancellation Policies:** Before booking, review the cruise line's cancellation and refund policies, as plans are subject to change.

Travel Arrangements:

- **Flights:** Schedule your flights to and from the cruise port. Major cities including Bergen, Oslo, and Stavanger serve as typical departure locations.
- **Transfers:** Make arrangements for transportation from the airport to the cruise terminal. Many cruise lines provide transfer services; alternatively, you can take cabs or public transportation.
- **Pre-Cruise and Post-Cruise Stays:** Consider spending extra days in Norway before or after your cruise to see the cities and surrounding areas more completely.

What to Pack: Essentials for your Cruise

Packing for a Norwegian fjords cruise takes careful consideration of the changing weather and the variety of activities available. The following are tips on essentials to pack for your cruise:

Clothing

- **Layers:** Pack layers to adjust to shifting temperatures. Include thermal undergarments, t-shirts, sweaters, and a waterproof jacket.
- **Footwear:** Good walking shoes are needed for exploring ports and trekking. Waterproof boots are suitable for rainy days.
- **Formal Attire:** Some cruises feature formal nights, so check to see if you need to bring a suit or cocktail dress.

Accessories

- **Binoculars:** Great for observing wildlife and admiring the sights from the ship.
- **Camera:** Capture the stunning view with a good camera and enough memory cards.
- **Daypacks:** Daypacks are useful for transporting essentials on seaside trips and hiking.

Health and Comfort

- **Motion Sickness Remedies:** Even if you don't feel seasick very often, it's a good idea to have some medicines on hand because

fjord cruises might occasionally meet rough waters.
- **Sunscreen and sunglasses:** Keep yourself safe from the sun, which may be harsh even on cloudy days.
- **Medications:** Bring necessary medications, as onboard medical services may not have precise prescriptions.

Embarkation: What to Expect

Embarkation is the process of boarding your cruise ship, and knowing what to expect can help make it go more smoothly and without stress.

Check-in Process

- **Documentation:** Make sure you have all of the appropriate travel documentation, such as your passport, cruise tickets, and any visas or health declarations.
- **Luggage Handling:** Your luggage is normally collected at the terminal and delivered to your cabin. Pack a carry-on with

essentials for the first day, as luggage delivery may take several hours.
- **Security Screening:** Before boarding the ship, you will be screened, similar to how you would at an airport.

CHAPTER TWO

Getting There and Around

A cruise through the Norwegian fjords necessitates extensive planning and consideration of travel logistics. From choosing the most convenient method of transportation to learning the subtleties of local travel, getting to your embarkation point and exploring the Norwegian fjords is an essential aspect of your adventure. This chapter explains how to get to Norway, travel to your cruise departure port, and explore the breathtaking fjord vistas while you're there.

Reaching Norway

Most Norwegian fjord cruises leave from big cities such as Bergen, Oslo, and Stavanger. Each of these cities are well-connected internationally, making Norway accessible from all around the world.

By Air:
- **Bergen Airport (BGO):**
  Bergen is often referred to as the "Gateway to the Fjords" and is a popular starting point for fjord tours. Airlines including SAS, Norwegian Air Shuttle, and Widerøe provide direct flights to Bergen from major European cities. From the United States, connecting flights are available through major hubs such as Amsterdam, London, and Copenhagen. The estimated cost of a round-trip flight from New York to Bergen is between $600 to $1,200, depending on the season and booking time.

- **Oslo Airport (OSL):**
  As Norway's major airport, Oslo provides numerous international connections, including direct flights from the United

States, Europe, and Asia. Airlines such as Norwegian Air Shuttle and SAS offer regular services at low prices and on numerous flights. Round-trip tickets from New York to Oslo normally cost between $600 to $1,000.

- **Stavanger Airport (SVG):**
  This airport is conveniently located near European cities and serves as a departure point for fjord cruises, although it is smaller than Bergen and Oslo. Flights from European cities such as London or Amsterdam to Stavanger typically cost $250 to $400 for a round trip.

By Sea:
- **Ferry Services:**
  For those traveling from surrounding European nations, consider taking a ferry. Services such as DFDS and Color Line provide routes from Denmark and Germany to Norway, providing a unique way to start your voyage with breathtaking views of the North Sea.

- **Price:** Ferry tickets can cost between €50 and €200 per person, depending on the route and cabin class.

Getting To The Cruise Departure Port

When you arrive in Norway, you must travel to the port where your cruise will depart. Here are several alternatives for transportation:

From Oslo to Bergen:
- **By Train:**
    Traveling by train from Oslo to Bergen offers breathtaking views of mountains and fjords,

making it one of Europe's most scenic routes. The Bergen Railway, operated by Vy, has multiple daily departures.
- **Price:** Tickets range from NOK 1,600 to NOK 2,600 (roughly $150 to $240), depending on the class and booking time.

- **By Plane:**
Domestic flights from Oslo to Bergen are frequent and take approximately an hour.
- **Price:** Tickets typically cost between NOK 1300 to NOK 3800 (about $120 to $350).

- **By Bus:**
Norway Bus express offers cost-effective long-distance bus services to connect cities.
- **Price:** Tickets cost between NOK 540 and NOK 1,000 (around $50 to $100).

From Oslo to Stavanger:
- **By Train:**
The 8-hour train ride from Oslo to Stavanger offers stunning views of the Norwegian countryside.

- **Price:** Ticket prices range from NOK 400 to NOK 1,200 (about $40 to $120).
- **By Plane:**
Traveling by plane from Oslo to Stavanger takes approximately 55 minutes.
- **Price:** Round-trip prices typically range between NOK 1,600 and NOK 2,700 (about $150 to $250).

Navigating The Fjords

Once you've embarked on your cruise, exploring the fjords becomes the highlight of your trip. However, many cruises allow you to disembark and explore the area around the fjords.

Onboard Excursions:
Most cruise lines have a choice of shore excursions that allow you to experience the fjords up close. These excursions frequently include guided tours, hikes, and visits to cultural places.

Hiking Excursions:
Popular hiking sites include Pulpit Rock (Preikestolen) and Trolltunga, which provide stunning views of the surrounding fjords.
Price: Guided hikes cost from NOK 500 to NOK 1,500 (about $50 to $150).

Cultural Tours:
Cultural tours include visits to local communities like Flåm and Geiranger to enjoy traditional Norwegian culture and cuisine.
Price: Tours are normally priced between NOK 400 to NOK 1,000 (about $40 to $100).

Kayaking and Boat Tours:
Kayaking in the fjords provides a unique opportunity to explore secret coves and waterfalls.
Price: Kayak rentals and guided tours cost between NOK 300 and NOK 800 (around $30 to $80).

Independent Exploration

For independent exploration, consider the following transportation choices and recommendations for navigating the fjords:

Rental Cars:

Renting a car allows you to explore the fjords at your own speed, stopping at scenic spots and attractions along the way.

Price: Rental rates start around NOK 500 per day (about $50), excluding petrol.

Public Transportation:

Norway's public transportation system is efficient, with buses and ferries linking major towns and fjords. Consider purchasing a "Norway in a Nutshell" trip ticket, which includes rail, bus, and boat travel for a unique fjord experience.

Price: The "Norway in a Nutshell" tour is priced between NOK 1,500 and NOK 2,500 (roughly $150 to $250), depending on the route and season.

Bicycles:
Bicycles provide an eco-friendly and active way to explore the fjord region, with various trails offering breathtaking views.
Price: Bicycles rentals range from NOK 150 to NOK 300 per day (about $15 to $30).

Tips For Navigating The Fjords

Weather Considerations:
The weather in the fjords is unpredictable. Pack layered clothing and wet items to keep comfortable on excursions.

Local Etiquette:
Norwegians are known for being polite and respectful of nature. Always adhere to established routes, dispose of rubbish responsibly, and respect local customs.

Sustainable Travel:
Norway promotes sustainable travel, encouraging travelers to reduce their environmental impact.

Consider driving an electric vehicle, taking public transportation, and supporting local businesses to promote environmentally responsible travel.

CHAPTER THREE

Accommodation On Board

Choosing the correct accommodation on your Norwegian fjords cruise is critical to having a relaxing and pleasurable vacation. Cruise lines provide a number of cabin types, each with its own set of features and facilities, to accommodate a wide range of preferences and budget. This chapter gives a comprehensive reference to understanding accommodations on a cruise, including information on cabin categories, what to anticipate from each, and insights into pricing.

Cabin Types and Categories

Cruise ships include a variety of cabin options, which are essentially classified into four categories: interior, ocean view, balcony, and suite. Each category offers varying levels of comfort, facilities, and price.

Interior Cabins

Interior cabins are the most cost-effective alternative and are located within the ship's interior, without windows or direct views of the water. They are great for budget-conscious travelers who prefer to spend their time visiting the ship and destinations rather than looking at stateroom views.

Features:
- **Size:** Ranges from 120 to 180 square feet.
- **Amenities:** comfortable beds, an en-suite bathroom with a shower, a television, a safe, and basic toiletries.
- **Additional features:** Some newer ships have virtual windows or portholes that provide real-time views from the outside.

- **Pricing:**
  Interior cabins on a Norwegian fjords cruise range from $500 to $1,200 per person for a seven-day cruise, depending on the cruise line, ship, and season.

Ocean View Cabins

Ocean view cabins have a window or porthole that lets in natural light and affords a view of the sea or ports. These accommodations are slightly more expensive than inside cabins but provide a sense of connection with the water.

Features:
- **Size:** Generally 150 to 200 square feet.
- **Amenities:** Similar to internal cabins, but with a window and a seating area by it.
- **View:** Depending on the cabin's position, vistas may be blocked or partially obscured.

- **Pricing:**
  Prices for ocean view cabins on 7-day cruises range from $700 to $1,500 per person, depending on ship age, cruise operator, and season.

Balcony Cabins

Balcony cabins are popular for their private outdoor space, which allows visitors to enjoy panoramic views and fresh sea air right from their accommodation. They provide a more opulent experience and are frequently the favored option for scenic areas such as the Norwegian fjords.

Features:

- **Size:** Usually 200-300 square feet, including the balcony.
- **Amenities:** Standard amenities, with additional outside seating on the balcony.
- **Experience:** Perfect for individual relaxation and viewing the breathtaking fjord landscapes.

- **Pricing:**
  Balcony suites range from $1,000 to $2,500 per person on a 7-day cruise. Prices vary depending on the cabin's position on the ship, the time of year, and the cruise line.

Suites

Suites are the most opulent accommodations aboard cruise ships, providing ample living space, premium amenities, and customized services. They are ideal for travelers looking for an enhanced cruise experience.

Features:

- **Size:** Ranges from 300 to over 1,500 square feet for the larger suites.
- **Amenities:** include separate living and sleeping rooms, huge balconies, premium furnishings, enhanced bathing facilities, and extras like a butler or concierge service.
- **Exclusive Access:** Suite guests may have access to the ship's most exclusive facilities, such as private lounges and dining areas.
- **Pricing:** Suite prices can range from $2,500 to over $10,000 per person on a 7-day cruise. The price is determined by the size of the suite, its location, and the individual amenities given.

Considerations For Choosing A Cabin

When choosing a cabin, consider the following things to ensure it suits your needs and tastes:

Budget:
Create a budget that covers the overall cost of the trip, including lodging, food, excursions, and other expenses. Remember that the choice of cabin has a considerable impact on the final cost.

Travel Style:
Decide how much time you want to spend in your cabin versus doing onboard activities and excursions. If you want to spend a lot of time admiring the scenery from your hotel, investing in a balcony cabin or suite may be worthwhile.

Location on the ship:
Cabins near the middle of the ship and on lower decks are frequently less motion-prone, which might be useful for seasick passengers. Consider your preferred location to elevators, dining areas, and other amenities.

Onboard Dining Options:

Dining options may be influenced by the kind of accommodation chosen, as some cruise lines have unique dining places for suite guests. However, all guests often have access to a number of food options:

Main Dining Room Experience:

Offers a variety of food options, including fixed seating hours and flexible dining arrangements. The main dining area delivers a formal dining experience at no additional expense.

- **Buffet:**
  A self-service alternative with a diverse selection of international cuisine and themes. Buffets are convenient for quick meals and may accommodate a wide range of tastes.

- **Specialty Restaurants:**
  Specialty restaurants provide distinctive dining experiences, such as steakhouses, Italian trattorias, and sushi bars. Reservations are frequently required for specialty meals, which also incurs additional expenses.

- **Casual Eateries and Cafés:**
  Casual dining establishments such as pizzerias, burger restaurants, and cafés serve lighter meals and snacks throughout the day.

Onboard Activities and Entertainment

The accommodation you select may also provide various bonuses relating to onboard activities and entertainment.

Entertainment

Theater events, live music, comedy performances, and movies are among the entertainment options available on board cruise liners. These events are often included in the cruise fare and offer evening entertainment to all guests.

Recreational Activities

Fitness centers, sports courts, and spas are offered to guests, while some cruise lines include unusual amenities such as rock climbing walls, water parks, or ice skating rinks.

Enrichment Programs

Many cruise lines offer educational and cultural events, such as guest lectures, cooking courses, and art workshops, to enhance the onboard experience and provide insight into the countries visited.

Cabin Services and Amenities

The level of service and amenities available in your stateroom may differ depending on the category and cruise line:

- **Housekeeping:**
  Regular housekeeping services ensure cabins are clean and neat throughout the voyage, including turndown service in the evening.

- **Room Service:**
  Most cruise lines provide room service, with some free and others asking a small price. Room service menus vary, allowing for in-cabin dining at any time.

- **Technology:**
  Cabins are outfitted with televisions, phones, and, in many cases, Wi-Fi (typically for a cost). Some luxury cabins and suites may

include additional technology features, such as in-room tablets or smart televisions.

CHAPTER FOUR

Ports of Call and Excursions

The ports of call on a Norwegian fjord cruise allow passengers to immerse themselves in Norway's natural beauty, cultural legacy, and local flavors. Each port offers its own set of activities and excursions that emphasize the region's breathtaking scenery and rich customs. This chapter looks at some of the most popular ports of call on a Norwegian fjord cruise, as well as recommended excursions that offer remarkable experiences.

Bergen: Gateway to the Fjords

Bergen, often the starting or ending location of many fjord cruises, is a bustling city surrounded by mountains and sea. As Norway's second largest city, Bergen is a UNESCO World Heritage site famed for its gorgeous waterfront, Bryggen.

Key Attractions:
- **Bryggen:** This historic Hanseatic dock is a tangle of narrow lanes and brightly painted wooden structures. It is an excellent location for visiting stores, cafes, and museums that highlight Bergen's rich maritime past.

- **Mount Fløyen:** Taking the Fløibanen funicular to the top of Mount Fløyen offers panoramic views of the city and neighboring fjords. The location has great hiking paths and a restaurant with spectacular views.

- **Bergen Fish Market:** A lively marketplace where you may try fresh fish, including local delicacies like king crab and smoked salmon.

Recommended Excursions:
- **Walking Tour of Bergen:** A guided tour of Bergen's historic core, including stops at Bryggen, St. Mary's Church, and the Rosenkrantz Tower.

- **Fjord Safari:** A high-speed RIB boat excursion around the neighboring fjords, providing close-up views of the breathtaking scenery and wildlife.

- **Art and Culture Tour:** Visit the KODE art museums, which have an excellent collection of Norwegian and foreign art, including paintings by Edvard Munch.

Geirangerfjord, Nature's Masterpiece

Geirangerfjord, one of Norway's most famous fjords, is known for its stunning scenery, including towering cliffs, gushing waterfalls, and lush green landscapes. This UNESCO World Heritage Site features some of the most spectacular fjord views.

Key Attractions:
- **Seven Sisters Waterfall:** This remarkable waterfall is made up of seven different streams that drop into the fjord from enormous heights. The best views are from

the ocean, but you can also see them from several vantage points around the fjord.

- **Eagle Road:** This is a winding road that ascends the steep mountainside, providing amazing views of Geirangerfjord from the summit.

- **Flydalsjuvet:** This is a popular viewpoint that offers an iconic view over the fjord and the municipality of Geiranger.

Recommended Excursions:
- **Kayaking in Geirangerfjord:** Paddle across the calm waters of the fjord, getting up close to waterfalls and breathtaking landscapes.

- **Hiking to Skageflå Farm**: A challenging hike to an abandoned mountain farm with panoramic views of the Geirangerfjord.

- **Geiranger Skywalk in Dalsnibba:** This viewing platform, 1,500 meters above sea level, provides a unique perspective of the fjord.

Flåm: A Village of Natural Wonders

Flåm, located at the end of Aurlandsfjord, a branch of the Sognefjord, is a picturesque settlement surrounded by tall mountains and deep valleys. It serves as a gateway to many of the region's most picturesque attractions.

Key Attractions:
- **The Flåm Railway:** One of the world's steepest train rides that provides a picturesque excursion through stunning scenery, including waterfalls, snow-capped peaks, and verdant valleys.

- **Naerøyfjord:** A UNESCO World Heritage site, is noted for its natural beauty and quiet surroundings.
- **Aurland Lookout (Stegastein):** A beautiful viewing platform that extends out over the fjord and provides unsurpassed views of the surrounding area.

Recommended Excursions
- **Flåm Railway and Fjord Cruise:** Combine a train ride on the Flåm Railway with a cruise on the Nærøyfjord for an amazing adventure.

- **Viking Valley Tour:** Visit the Njardarheimr Viking Village in Gudvangen to experience life as it was during the Viking Age.

- **Electric Bike Tour:** ‚Explore the gorgeous surroundings of Flåm on an electric bike tour, which includes routes through quaint villages and along the fjord.

Stavanger: A Combination of Old and New

Stavanger is a dynamic city that blends historical charm with modern vigor. It is noted for its attractive old town, dynamic cultural environment, and closeness to some of Norway's most well-known natural features.

Key Attractions:
- **Old Stavanger:** Walk through Europe's best-preserved wooden house community, with tiny alleyways lined with white wooden buildings and blossoming flowers.

- **The Norwegian Petroleum Museum:** Explore the history of Norway's oil industry and its impact on the country's economy and society.

- **Stavanger Church:** Norway's oldest church, completed in the 12th century, features stunning Romanesque and Gothic architecture.

Recommended Excursions:
- **Hike to Pulpit Rock (Preikestolen):** Pulpit Rock is a popular hiking site with breathtaking views of the Lysefjord from its flat-topped bluff.

- **Lysefjord Cruise:** Take a boat cruise through the stunning landscapes of Lysefjord, which features towering cliffs and flowing waterfalls.

- **Kjerag Boulder Hike:** For the daring, hike to the Kjerag Boulder, a massive stone jammed between two cliffs that provides a spectacular photo opportunity.

Ålesund: An Art Nouveau Gem

Ålesund, on Norway's west coast, is renowned for its unique Art Nouveau buildings and picturesque coastline environment. The city is spread out among various islands, providing stunning views of the surrounding sea and mountains.

Key Attractions:
- **Aksla Viewpoint:** Climb Mount Aksla's 418 steps to enjoy panoramic views of Ålesund and nearby islands.

- **Jugendstilsenteret:** The Art Nouveau Center highlights Ålesund's architectural heritage and provides historical context.

- **Ålesund Aquarium**: One of Northern Europe's largest aquariums, showcasing a diverse range of marine life from the Norwegian coast.

Recommended Excursions:

- **Guided City Tour:** Discover Ålesund's Art Nouveau architecture and learn about its history and culture on a walking tour.

- **Bird Watching on Runde Island:** Runde Island has significant bird colonies, including puffins, guillemots, and kittiwakes.

- **Sunnmøre Alps Hiking:** Experience the breathtaking peaks and valleys of the Sunnmøre Alps on a guided hiking tour.

CHAPTER FIVE

Dining and Cuisine

Dining in Norway is a rich and tasty adventure that celebrates the country's cultural heritage, copious natural resources, and commitment to sustainability. As you cruise through the Norwegian fjords, you will be able to enjoy a wide range of culinary pleasures both on board and at numerous ports of call. This chapter delves into the culinary experiences you can expect on a Norwegian fjord cruise, including classic Norwegian dishes, regional delicacies, and the distinct flavors that define Norwegian food.

The Foundation of Norwegian Cuisine

Norwegian cuisine is firmly anchored in the country's natural surroundings and historical practices. The diet is heavily impacted by Norway's extensive coastline, enormous woods, and harsh mountains, which give an abundance of ingredients. Seafood is a staple, with the cold, clean seas of the North Atlantic producing some of the world's best fish and shellfish. The quantity of fertile land, as well as the agricultural and foraging traditions, all contribute to the variety of ingredients utilized in Norwegian cuisine.

Key Ingredients:

- **Seafood:** Salmon, cod, herring, mackerel, and shellfish are the highlights of Norwegian cuisine. Freshness and quality are crucial, with seafood being consumed smoked, cured, or simply prepared to showcase its natural qualities.

- **Meat and Game:** Lamb, hog, and beef are popular foods, often prepared in traditional ways such as roasting or curing. Reindeer, elk, and grouse are popular game meats in particular places, reflecting Norway's hunting traditions.

- **Dairy:** Norway produces high-quality dairy products such as butter, cream, and a large selection of cheeses, the most well-known of which is brunost, a caramelized brown cheese.

- **Berries & Fruits**: The country's forests and fields provide a plethora of berries, including lingonberries, cloudberries, and blueberries, which are used in sweets, jams, and sauces.

- **Root vegetables and grains:** Potatoes, carrots, turnips, and cabbage are common vegetables that are eaten alongside fish and meat meals. Bread and porridge are made from grains like barley, oats, and rye.

Traditional Norwegian Dishes

Throughout your trip, you will sample a selection of traditional Norwegian meals that highlight the country's culinary heritage. These recipes highlight the simplicity and quality of Norwegian ingredients, which are typically prepared with minimal spice to allow the natural tastes to emerge.

Fiskesuppe (fish soup)

A creamy, warming soup cooked with a mix of fish and shellfish, typically salmon and cod. It is seasoned with fresh herbs and vegetables, with cream added on occasion.

Raspeballer (potato dumplings)

These traditional dumplings are made with grated potatoes and flour, then boiled and served with salty meats, sausages, or root vegetables.

Smørbrød (open-faced sandwiches)

These sandwiches, a Norwegian dining classic, are made with buttered bread and topped with cured meats, smoked salmon, cheese, and pickled vegetables.

Pinnekjøtt: Salted lamb ribs

Pinnekjøtt, a traditional Christmas dish, includes salted and dried lamb ribs boiled over birch branches for a unique flavor.

Klippfisk (dry and salted cod)

This meal features cod that has been dried and salted, then rehydrated and prepared in a variety of ways, including stews and casseroles. It is a staple in coastal areas and represents Norway's ancient tradition of preserving fish.

Kjøttkaker (Meatballs)

Kjøttkaker, like Swedish meatballs, are made with ground beef or a combination of meats, seasoned, and served with gravy, potatoes, and lingonberry sauce.

Five Budget-Friendly Restaurants in the Norwegian Fjords

Pingvinen, Bergen

Why Dine Here?
Pingvinen is a charming and popular gastropub in the heart of Bergen. Pingvinen is known for serving authentic Norwegian comfort food in a calm setting with pleasant service.

Cuisine:

The menu offers typical Norwegian cuisine, like meatballs (kjøttkaker), fish soup (fiskesuppe), and lamb stew (fårikål). Portions are generous, and costs are affordable, making it popular with both residents and tourists.

Highlights:

- Cozy and rustic interior with a welcoming vibe.
- A diverse assortment of local beers and ciders.
- Seasonal cuisine made with fresh, local ingredients.
- Vegetarian and Gluten-Free Options.

- **Meals:.** Lunch, Dinner, Brunch, Late Night.

- **Qualities:** Seating, Available highchairs, Accessible wheelchair, Accepts American Express, Mastercard, Visa, Credit Cards, and has free WiFi and Table Service.

- **Average Price Range:**
The average price range for main courses is NOK 75–269 ($7–25).

Bryggeloftet and Stuene, Bergen

Why Dine Here?

Bryggeloftet and Stuene, located along the historic Bryggen wharf, provides a taste of traditional Norwegian cuisine in a picturesque environment. The restaurant has served Bergen since 1910, offering a diverse gastronomic experience at a reasonable price.

Cuisine:

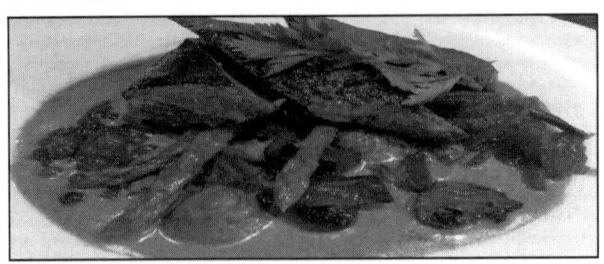

Expect traditional Norwegian cuisine such as herring, fish, and venison. The restaurant also has a daily special, which is frequently a good deal for budget-conscious diners.

Highlights:

- Historic position overlooking the UNESCO-listed Bryggen.
- Traditional interior reflecting Bergen's cultural past.
- Focuses on locally supplied fish and game.
- Vegetarian, Vegan, and Gluten-Free Options

- **Meals:** Lunch, Dinner, Brunch, Late Night.

- **Qualities:** Outdoor seating, private dining, Available Highchairs, Full bar, Accepts Credit Cards, Has Table Service, Family Style setting, and Available Gift Cards.

- **Average Price Range:** The average price range for main courses is NOK 160–960 ($15–$90).

Kafé Kremmergaarden (Ålesund)

Why Dine Here?
Kafé Kremmergaarden inn Ålesund offers courteous service and homemade cuisine at cheap costs. This cafe is an excellent place to have a quick dinner or a sweet treat while touring the gorgeous town.

Cuisine:

Menu Highlights:

- **Bacalao (a Norwegian cod dish):** Made with tomatoes, olives, and potatoes.
- Reindeer stew is served with mashed potatoes and lingonberries.
- A variety of sandwiches and handmade cakes.
- **Meals:** Lunch, Dinner, Brunch, Late Night.
- **Qualities:** Seating, Available highchairs, Accessible wheelchair, Accepts American Express, Mastercard, Visa, Credit Cards, and has free WiFi.
- **Average Price Range:**
  Price range for main courses and sandwiches is 20-180 NOK ($2-$17).

The Flåm Marina and Appartement Café

Why Dine Here?

Located by the Aurlandsfjord in Flåm, this cafe provides spectacular views and a variety of good and affordable Norwegian food. It is an excellent choice for travelers wishing to enjoy a dinner against a gorgeous environment.

Cuisine:

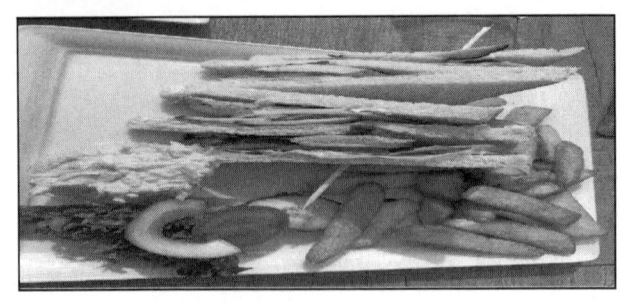

Menu Highlights:

- Open-faced sandwiches with shrimp, smoked salmon, or cured meats.
- Norwegian waffles, served with sour cream and jam.
- **Seafood chowder:** prepared with local fish and shellfish.

- **Meals:** Lunch, Dinner, Brunch, drinks

- **Qualities:** Available highchairs, Accessible wheelchair Outdoor seating, Reservations, Table service and free WiFi.

- **Average Price Range:** Light lunches and larger courses normally range from 129 to 230 NOK ($12 to $22).

Tre Brør Café, Voss

Why Dine Here?
Tre Brør Café in Voss offers a relaxed atmosphere and a choice of Norwegian and international cuisine. It's a favorite among budget-conscious travelers, thanks to its friendly setting and devotion to using locally grown ingredients.

Cuisine:

Menu Highlights:

- Lamb burger with locally sourced meat and traditional toppings.
- A vegetarian curry with seasonal veggies and rice.
- Daily specials with locally sourced ingredients.
- Gluten Free Options.
- **Meals:** Lunch, Dinner, Brunch, Late Night.
- **Qualities:** Available highchairs, Accessible wheelchair Outdoor seating, Reservations Full Bar, Takeouts, Table service, Accepts American Express, Mastercard, Visa, Credit Cards, and has free WiFi.
- **Average Price Range:** Main meals range from 107 to 260 NOK ($10-25).

These budget-friendly restaurants provide a taste of real Norwegian cuisine while allowing you to experience the breathtaking fjord vistas without breaking the bank. Whether in Bergen, Voss, Flåm, or Ålesund, you'll discover great and affordable selections to fit your taste.

CHAPTER SIX

Events and Festivals

Norway is a country rich in culture, history, and natural beauty, and its events and festivals reflect its lively legacy. The festivals in Norwegian fjords are as diverse as the terrain, allowing visitors to immerse themselves in local traditions, music, food, and art. There is something for everyone, whether you want to see historical reenactments, hear music, or eat delicious food. This chapter discusses some of the most significant events and festivals in the fjord regions, highlighting their importance and what visitors might expect.

National Celebrations

Norwegian Constitution Day (May 17th):
Constitution Day, or "Syttende Mai," is Norway's national holiday that commemorates the signing of the Norwegian Constitution in 1814. This is one of the most important and highly celebrated events in the country, with festivities taking place in cities and towns all along the fjords.

- **Parades and Processions:**
  The colorful parades on Constitution Day feature children dressed in traditional costumes (bunads), marching bands, and banners. Cities such as Bergen and Stavanger host massive parades involving thousands of people.

- **Cultural Performances:**
  Throughout the day, you can watch traditional Norwegian music, dance, and theatrical performances that highlight the country's rich cultural heritage.

- **Family Gatherings:**
  Norwegians celebrate with family picnics and parties, when they enjoy traditional meals like smoked salmon, cured meats, and waffles.

Midsummer Celebration (June 23):

Midsummer, or "Jonsok" as it is known in Norway, commemorates the summer solstice and is a time for communities to gather and enjoy the long daylight hours.

- **Bonfires:**
  One of the most recognizable aspects of Midsummer is the lighting of massive bonfires along the fjords, which represent the sun and drive away evil spirits.

- **Folk Music and Dance:**
  Traditional folk music and dance performances take place, with people converging to hear live bands and participate in circle dances.

Outdoor Feasts:
Communities frequently host outdoor feasts that include fresh local fruit, grilled meats, and seasonal desserts.

Music and Art Festivals

- **Bergen International Festival (May to June):**
Bergen International Festival is one of the largest and most distinguished arts festivals in the Nordic region. It brings together international talents for two weeks of performances in music, theater, dance, and visual arts.

- **Concerts:**
The festival features an excellent roster of performances spanning from classical and opera to jazz and contemporary music, all performed in historic settings like the Grieg Hall and Bergen Cathedral.

- **Theater and Dance:**

International theater and dance organizations demonstrate their talents with a broad program of both contemporary and classic performances.

- **Art Exhibitions:**
Art enthusiasts can view exhibitions by renowned and new artists, with a focus on contemporary and traditional works.

Førde Traditional and World Music Festival (July):

This festival, held in Førde, Sognefjord, celebrates traditional and international music, attracting musicians and fans from all over the world.

- **World-Class Performances:**
The festival showcases a wide range of musical forms, including folk, roots, and ethnic music, which are performed in concert halls, churches, and outdoor venues.

- **Workshops and Seminars:**
Attendees can take part in workshops and seminars led by musicians, which provide

insights into various musical traditions and approaches.

- **Cultural Experiences:**
  The festival also features dance workshops, art exhibitions, and culinary experiences, ensuring a complete cultural immersion.

Nattjazz Festival (May to June):
Nattjazz, held in Bergen, is one of Europe's longest-running jazz events, attracting prominent international and Norwegian jazz musicians.

- **Live Jazz Performances:**
  Over ten nights, the festival presents a broad program of jazz performances, ranging from traditional to experimental, in intimate locations throughout the city.

- **Collaborations and Jam Sessions:**
  Musicians frequently collaborate to create unique, one-of-a-kind performances, while jam sessions encourage spontaneous musical innovation.

- **Workshops:**
Jazz aficionados can attend workshops and masterclasses led by experienced performers to improve their understanding and appreciation of the genre.

Historical and Cultural Festivals

Viking Festivals

Norway's Viking legacy is celebrated in a variety of events around the fjord regions, giving tourists a glimpse into the country's illustrious history.

- **The Avaldsnes Viking Festival (June):** Located on the island of Karmøy in Haugesund, this festival features historical markets, battle exhibitions, and storytelling sessions. Visitors can visit authentic Viking encampments and take part in traditional crafts and activities.

- **Gudvangen Viking Market (July):** Located in the gorgeous Naerøyfjord, this market draws Viking aficionados from all over the world. It includes a lively marketplace with craftsmen selling homemade goods, along with Viking fights, music, and feasting.

Røros Winter Fair (February):
The Røros Winter Fair, also known as "Rørosmartnan," is a traditional fair that has been held in the UNESCO World Heritage town of Røros since 1854.

- **Market Vendors:**
  With over 250 vendors selling local crafts, food, and merchandise, the fair provides a one-of-a-kind shopping experience in the old town center.

- **Traditional Activities:**
  Traditional activities include horse-drawn sleigh rides, folk music performances, and exhibitions of traditional crafts.

- **Cultural Events:**
  The fair hosts a number of cultural events, including storytelling sessions, theatrical performances, and art exhibitions.

Food and Beverage Festivals

- **Gladmat Food Festival (July):** Stavanger hosts the Gladmat culinary Festival, one of Scandinavia's major culinary events, which draws foodies and chefs from all over the world.

- **Culinary Delights:** The festival celebrates Norway's culinary diversity, with vendors selling everything from traditional meals to new gourmet inventions.

- **Cooking Demonstrations:** Renowned chefs give cooking demonstrations and seminars to share their knowledge and inspire home cooks.

- **Tasting Events:** Attendees can take part in tasting events including local specialties, fresh seafood, and creative meals.

Nordic Beer Festival, September:
The Nordic Beer Festival, held in Bergen, highlights the region's booming craft beer culture, including

brewers from all around the Nordics displaying their creations.

- **Beer Tastings:**
Visitors can try a wide range of beers, including conventional ales and lagers as well as inventive brews made with unique ingredients.

- **Breweries and Taprooms:**
The festival focuses on local breweries and taprooms, providing insights into the brewing process and opportunities to meet the brewers.

- **Food Pairings:**
Beer and food pairings are a popular feature, with local chefs crafting dishes that compliment the flavors of various beers.

Seasonal and Outdoor Events

- **Northern Lights Festivals (Winter):**
Norway's winter months provide a beautiful experience with the Northern Lights, which are celebrated at various festivals.

- **The Tromsø International Film Festival (January):**
This festival in January combines culture and nature by offering Northern Lights viewing tours.

- **Tromso Northern Lights Festival (January):**
This is a music festival featuring classical and contemporary acts against the backdrop of the aurora borealis.

Outdoor Adventure Events:
Norway's spectacular landscapes make an ideal venue for outdoor adventure events and competitions.

- **Norwegian Fjord Marathon (August):**
This marathon, held in the breathtaking backdrop of the fjords, draws runners from all over the world. Participants can select between several distances, including a full marathon, a half marathon, and shorter races.

- **Extreme Sports Week (June):** Held in Voss, this event is Europe's largest extreme sports festival, with activities including skydiving, paragliding, whitewater rafting, and climbing. Spectators can watch the adrenaline-fueled action while also participating in workshops and activities.

CHAPTER SEVEN

Practical Information

When organizing a cruise through the Norwegian fjords, having access to practical knowledge can substantially improve your experience and ensure a pleasant vacation. This chapter provides a complete reference to the crucial things you need to know before setting sail, including understanding the local currency and language, knowing what to carry, and how to stay connected.

Currency and Payment Methods

- **Currency:**
  Norway's official currency is the Norwegian Krone (NOK). While credit and debit cards are generally accepted, it is best to carry cash for smaller shops, rural locations, and public transit, where card payments may not be available.

- **Currency Denomination:**
  Banknotes are issued in denominations of 50, 100, 200, 500, and 1,000 NOK. Coins come in denominations of one, five, ten, and twenty NOK.

- **Currency Exchange:**
  Currency can be exchanged at airports, banks and currency exchange offices in Norway. ATMs are also commonly available, with competitive exchange rates.

Payment Methods:
- **Credit and Debit Cards:**
Visa and MasterCard are commonly accepted in Norway, including most hotels, restaurants, and businesses. American Express is less widely recognized, so a Visa or MasterCard is a good backup.

- **Mobile Payments:**
Norway leads the way in mobile payment solutions, with systems such as Vipps frequently utilized for transactions. If you intend to use mobile payment methods, be sure your phone is configured to accept foreign payments.

Language and Communication

Official Language:
Norwegian is the official language in Norway, with two written forms: Bokmål and Nynorsk. Bokmål is the most extensively used language, particularly in urban areas. English is commonly spoken, especially in tourist regions, and the majority of Norwegians are fluent in English.

Useful Phrases:

While English is widely spoken, learning a few basic Norwegian words will enrich your experience and demonstrate respect for the local culture. Here are some useful phrases:

- **Hello:** Hei.
- **Please:** Vær så snill.
- **Thank you:** Takk.
- **Yes:** Ja.
- **No:** Nei.

Communication:

- **Internet and Wi-Fi:**

    Wi-Fi is readily available in hotels, cafes, and public areas. Wi-Fi is also available on cruise ships, though it may be limited and come at an additional cost.

- **Mobile Roaming:**

    Ask your mobile operator about foreign roaming alternatives. If you expect to use your phone frequently, consider acquiring a local SIM card for data and calls.

Health and Safety

- **Health Care:**
Norway provides high-quality healthcare facilities, including well-equipped hospitals and clinics in major cities and towns. Emergency medical services are available, however it is critical to obtain travel insurance that covers medical expenses, as healthcare in Norway can be expensive for non-residents.

- **Vaccinations:**
Travelers to Norway are not required to have any specific vaccinations, but normal vaccinations such as measles, mumps, rubella (MMR), diphtheria-tetanus-pertussis, and influenza are highly recommended.

Safety Tips:
- **Emergency Numbers:**
In Norway, the emergency number for police, ambulance, and fire services is 112.

- **Personal Safety:**
  Norway is one of the world's safest countries, with low crime rates. However, it is always advisable to take basic precautions, such as securing valuables and remaining aware of your surroundings.

Traveling With Children

Norway is a family-friendly destination, with several cruise lines providing amenities and activities specifically for children. Here are some tips for traveling with children:

- **Family-Friendly Activities:**
  Look for cruises that include kids' clubs, family excursions, and onboard activities such as swimming pools and entertainment.

- **Packing for Kids:**
  Bring extra clothing, snacks, and entertainment alternatives like books, games, and tablets for downtime during travel.

BONUS SECTION

Sample Itineraries

Seven-Day Norwegian Fjord Cruise Itinerary:
Embark on a 7-day trip through the spectacular Norwegian fjords, where stunning scenery, rich culture, and amazing adventures await. This tour visits some of the most renowned fjords and places of call, providing an ideal balance of picturesque cruising and interactive activities. Each day is meant to highlight the finest of Norway, from its natural beauties to its quaint villages and cultural traditions.

Day 1: Arrival at Bergen

- **Morning:**
  Arrive at Bergen, often known as the "Gateway to the Fjords." Explore the city's picturesque shoreline and the medieval Bryggen neighborhood, a UNESCO World Heritage Site. Wander through the small passageways and stop by the Hanseatic Museum to learn about Bergen's maritime heritage.

- **Afternoon:**
  Take the Fløibanen funicular to the top of Mount Fløyen for panoramic views of the city and nearby fjords. Take a trek along the picturesque paths or relax at the mountaintop café.

- **Evening:**
  Board the cruise ship and settle into your stateroom. As you set sail from Bergen, enjoy the welcome supper onboard and meet your other travelers.

Day 2: Geirangerfjord

- **Morning:**
  Arrive in Geiranger, home to the spectacular Geirangerfjord, a UNESCO World Heritage Site. Begin your day with a picturesque drive along the Eagle Road, stopping at the Ørnesvingen viewpoint to enjoy stunning views of the fjord and the Seven Sisters waterfall.
- **Afternoon:**
  Take a guided kayaking tour of Geirangerfjord, amid waterfalls and stunning cliffs. Hike to the abandoned mountain farm at Skageflå for spectacular views of the fjord.
- **Evening:**
  Return to the ship for a relaxed evening aboard. Enjoy a typical Norwegian supper that includes fresh seafood and local delights.

Day 3: Ålesund

- **Morning:**
 Dock in Ålesund, known for its Art Nouveau architecture. Explore the town's colorful buildings and visit the Jugendstilsenteret, or Art Nouveau Center, to learn about the town's architectural history.

- **Afternoon Activity:**
 Climb 418 steps to the Aksla viewpoint for panoramic views of Ålesund and nearby islands. After a relaxing lunch at a local cafe, take a boat tour to nearby Runde Island, which is famed for its vast seabird colonies, including puffins.

- **Evening:**
 Return aboard the ship to enjoy live music and entertainment. As you travel to your next location, relax on the deck with a cocktail.

Day 4: Geiranger and Hellesylt

- **Morning:**
  Arrive in Hellesylt, a lovely town at the head of the Sunnylvsfjorden. Explore the village and see the Hellesylt Waterfall, which cascades through the middle of town.

- **Afternoon:**
  Visit Jostedalsbreen National Park, which is home to mainland Europe's largest glacier. Hike the trails surrounding the Briksdal Glacier for a closer look at this magnificent ice feature.

- **Evening:**
  Return to the ship and have a leisurely meal while cruising through the tranquil waters of Geirangerfjord. Attend a lecture on Norway's natural history and culture, given by onboard specialists.

Day 5 : Olden and Nordfjord

- **Morning:**
  Dock in Olden, a lovely town on the innermost arm of Nordfjord. Take a tour of the Jostedalsbreen National Park, which includes the Briksdal Glacier. Travel by troll car or hike to the glacier to admire the breathtaking ice structures and surrounding scenery.

- **Afternoon:**
  Take the Loen Skylift, one of the world's steepest cable cars, for stunning views of the fjord and mountains. Enjoy a classic Norwegian meal at the mountaintop restaurant.

- **Evening:**
  Return to the ship and relax with a spa treatment, or spend a quiet evening on deck, admiring the fjord vistas as you sail to your next stop.

Day 6: Sognefjord & Flåm

- **Morning:**
  Arrive in Flåm, located at the end of Aurlandsfjord, a tributary of the Sognefjord. Board the Flåm Railway, one of the world's most scenic train trips, passing through magnificent scenery of mountains, waterfalls, and valleys.

- **Afternoon:**
  Explore the village of Flåm, see the local museum, and have a leisurely lunch in a cafe. Consider a RIB boat safari to explore the tiny and scenic Naerøyfjord.

- **Evening:**
  Return to the ship for a goodbye supper to commemorate the adventure with new friends. As you cruise back to Bergen, reflect on the magnificent sights and experiences you've had over the last week.

Day 7: Return to Bergen

- **Morning:**
  Arrive at Bergen and disembark from the cruise ship. Spend the morning seeing any remaining attractions in Bergen, such as the KODE art museums or the Bergen Aquarium.

- **Afternoon:**
  Have your final meal in Bergen's bustling city center, possibly eating some of the fresh fish at the famous Fish Market.

- **Evening:**
  Transfer to Bergen Airport for your departure, or continue seeing Norway with extra travel options.

This 7-day Norwegian fjord cruise itinerary provides a perfect blend of scenic cruising with immersive experiences, allowing you to discover the natural beauty and cultural richness of Norway's fjords.

Seasonal Recommendations

Seasonal Tips for a Norwegian Fjord Cruise:
Cruising the Norwegian fjords is an amazing experience, providing spectacular scenery and insight into Norway's rich cultural past. Each season in the fjords has its own particular beauty and opportunity for exploration, so it's critical to plan your trip around your interests and tastes. This guide provides comprehensive recommendations for visiting the Norwegian fjords throughout the year, highlighting the finest experiences and considerations for each season.

Spring (April to May):
Spring is an ideal time to visit the Norwegian fjords as nature awakens from its winter hibernation. The terrain is lush and green, with wildflowers blooming and waterfalls at their peak strength due to melting snow.

Highlights:
- **Blossoming Orchards:**
  The Hardangerfjord region is known for its fruit orchards, and spring is the best season to observe them in full bloom. The picture of

apple and cherry blossoms against a backdrop of snow-capped mountains is simply breathtaking.

- **Waterfalls:**
Spring is the greatest time to see the fjords' beautiful waterfalls, such as the Seven Sisters and Bridal Veil in Geirangerfjord, because they are fed by melting snow and at their peak.

- **Hiking:**
Trails start to open up, providing excellent hiking options. The temperature is cool yet appropriate for outdoor activities, and prominent trails are less crowded than during the summer.

Considerations:
- **Weather:** Spring weather in Norway can be unpredictable, with fluctuating temperatures and the occasional rain. To stay comfortable, pack layers and waterproof gear.

- **Crowds:** Spring is less crowded than summer, resulting in a more relaxing experience at major sights and attractions.

Summer (June-August):
Summer is the peak season for cruising the Norwegian fjords, with long daylight hours and warm temperatures. This is the ideal time for outdoor activities and discovering the area's natural beauties.

Highlights:
- **Midnight Sun:**
  In the northern fjords, you can witness the midnight sun phenomena, in which the sun is visible until midnight. This extra daylight gives you more time to explore and appreciate the environment.

- **Outdoor Activities:**
  The summer months are perfect for hiking, kayaking, and cycling in the fjords. Popular walks include those to Pulpit Rock and Trolltunga, which provide breathtaking panoramic vistas.

- **Cultural Activities:**
  Norway's cultural legacy is celebrated through summer events like the Bergen International Festival and the Førde Traditional and World Music Festival.

- **Wildlife Watching:**
  Because wildlife such as seals, porpoises, and numerous bird species are more active during the summer, it is the perfect time to observe them.

Considerations:

- **Crowds:** Because summer is the peak season for tourists, major sights and ports can become overcrowded. It is recommended that you schedule your trips and accommodations in advance.

- **Prices:** Summer is the peak season for cruises, accommodations, and activities, therefore prices are often higher.

Autumn (September-October):

Autumn in the Norwegian fjords is marked by magnificent fall foliage and a more peaceful environment as the summer throng disperse.

Highlights:
- **Fall Foliage:**
  The fjord landscapes are changed by bright autumn colors, creating a magnificent backdrop for photography and outdoor exploration.

- **Harvest Season:**
  Autumn is the harvest season in Norway, and local markets sell fresh products such as apples, berries, and mushrooms. This is an excellent time to sample Norwegian culinary delicacies.

- **Hiking and Outdoor Activities:**
  The weather stays favorable for outdoor activities, and the trails are less crowded, providing a more peaceful trekking experience.

- **Cultural Events:**
  The Lofoten International Art Festival and other cultural events take place in the autumn, offering a glimpse into Norway's current art scene.

Considerations:
- **Weather:** Autumn weather can be unpredictable, with colder temperatures and the likelihood of rainfall. Prepare with layers of clothing and rain gear.

- **Shorter Days:** As the season passes, daylight hours shorten, so arrange your activities accordingly to make the best use of the remaining light.

Winter (November – March):
Winter in the Norwegian fjords is a unique and magical experience, complete with snow-covered scenery and the opportunity to see the Northern Lights. This season is great for individuals who want a calmer, more intimate experience.

Highlights:
- **Northern Lights:**
  The winter months are the greatest time to see the Northern Lights, especially in the northern fjords. Clear, dark nights are best for seeing this natural occurrence.

- **Winter Sports:**
  The fjord regions of Norway are ideal for skiing, snowboarding, and snowshoeing.

- **Christmas Markets:**
  Festive Christmas markets pop up in Norwegian villages and cities, offering local goods, food, and seasonal pleasure.

- **Tranquility:**
  Winter is the off-season for tourists in the fjords, providing a more peaceful experience with fewer people and lower pricing.

Considerations:
- **Weather:** Winter temperatures can be cold, particularly in the north. Pack warm clothing

and layers to keep you comfortable during outdoor activities.

- **Limited Daylight:** Winter days are short, especially in December and January, so plan activities to make the most of the daylight.

- **Limited Accessibility:** Snow and ice may make some hikes and attractions inaccessible, so check local conditions and plan appropriately.

Choosing the optimum time to cruise the Norwegian fjords depends on your preferences and desired experiences. Each season has its own appeal and opportunity, from the vivid blossoms of spring to the limitless sunshine of summer, the colorful leaves of autumn, and the majestic Northern Lights of winter. By taking into account the highlights and considerations of each season, you can design a fjord cruise that is tailored to your interests and guarantees an amazing experience through one of the world's most breathtaking settings.

Basic Norwegian Phrases

Learning some basic Norwegian phrases can enhance your travel experience and help you connect with locals during your trip to the fjords. Here are 30 useful phrases and vocabulary in Norwegian for travelers:

Basic Greetings and Politeness:

- **Hei:** Hello.
- **God morgen**: Good morning.
- **God ettermiddag:** Good afternoon.
- **God kveld:** Good evening.
- **Ha det:** Goodbye.
- **Vær så snill:** Please.
- **Takk:** Thank you.
- **Tusen takk:** Thank you very much.
- **Unnskyld:** Excuse me.
- **Beklager:** I'm sorry.

Common Questions:

- **Hvordan har du det?** - How are you?
- **Hva heter du?** - What is your name?
- **Hvor er...?** - Where is...?
- **Kan du hjelpe meg?** - Can you help me?
- **Snakker du engelsk?** - Do you speak English?
- **Hvor mye koster det?** - How much does it cost?
- **Hva er klokka?** - What time is it?

Directions and Transportation:

- **Til høyre:** To the right.
- **Til venstre:** To the left.
- **Rett fram:** Straight ahead.
- **Hvor er nærmeste togstasjon?** – Where is the nearest train station?
- **Jeg trenger en taxi:** I need a taxi.
- **Kan jeg få en billett til...?** – Can I get a ticket to...?

Dining and Food:

- **Kan jeg få menyen, takk?** – Can I have the menu, please?
- **Jeg vil gjerne bestille...** – I would like to order...
- **Er dette vegetarisk?** – Is this vegetarian?
- **Kan jeg få regningen, takk?** – Can I have the bill, please?
- **Hva anbefaler du?** – What do you recommend?

Emergencies and Health:

- **Hjelp!** – Help!
- **Jeg trenger en lege** – I need a doctor.

These phrases cover a variety of situations that travelers may encounter and can help make your interactions smoother and more enjoyable. Learning a few words of the local language is always appreciated and can make your journey even more rewarding.

Shopping and Souvenirs in The Norwegian Fjords

Shopping in the Norwegian fjords provides an enjoyable opportunity to discover a wide range of one-of-a-kind products that reflect the region's cultural heritage, artistic workmanship, and natural beauty. From traditional handicrafts to gourmet delicacies, travelers can find a wide variety of gifts that embody the soul of Norway. Here's a guide to the top shopping and souvenir options in the fjords.

Traditional Handicrafts Knitwear and Woolen products:

Norwegian knitwear, particularly the classic Dale of Norway sweaters, is known for its superior quality and traditional designs. These clothing are not only warm and useful, but they also have intricate designs inspired by Norwegian folklore and environment. Woolen scarves, mittens, and socks are especially popular, bringing warm memories of your fjord journey.

- **Bunads:**

    The Bunad is a traditional Norwegian outfit used on special events and festivals. While a full bunad can be fairly expensive, many shops sell smaller products such as bunad-inspired jewelry, accessories, and embroidered textiles that make excellent mementos.

Local Arts and Crafts

- **Røros Pottery:**

    Røros is recognized for its unusual ceramics with hand-painted motifs reflecting the region's history and scenery. Visitors can purchase a variety of ceramic objects, including attractive plates and functional utensils.

- **Glass & Crystal:**

    Norway has several notable glassworks that produce magnificent handcrafted glass and crystal items. Hadeland Glassverk, near Oslo, sells a wide range of glass art, vases, and ornamental pieces that highlight the artistry of Norwegian glassmakers.

- **Wood Carvings:**

    Woodworking is a traditional craft in Norway, with talented artisans carving exquisite figures of trolls, animals, and scenes from Norwegian mythology. These hand-carved keepsakes are one-of-a-kind and authentic, capturing the essence of the fjords.

Practical Tips for Shopping

Tax-free shopping:

Visitors from outside Norway can enjoy tax-free shopping by recovering VAT on purchases made at participating stores. Look for the "Tax-Free Shopping" logo and retain your receipts to complete your refund at the airport when you depart.

Supporting Local Artists:

When shopping for souvenirs, consider supporting local artisans and craft cooperatives. Not only does this ensure product authenticity, but it also benefits the local economy and helps to maintain traditional crafts.

Shopping in the Norwegian fjords is a rewarding experience that allows you to bring home a piece of Norway's culture and craftsmanship. Whether you're seeking for traditional handicrafts, local art, or culinary delights, the fjords have a plethora of unique gifts to mark your trip through this gorgeous region.

Printed in Great Britain
by Amazon